Advance Pr

PREVAILING WINDS

*poems by*
# Joseph Stanton

"The range and precision of Joseph Stanton's *Prevailing Winds* is breathtaking. From ekphrases and portraits of the flora and fauna of Hawai'i (and beyond) to the unveiling of artists (of all stripes!) and the vitality simmering just below the surface of their work, each poem opens the reader to a new world—of color, of sound, of language, of meaning."

—GILBERT L. GIGLIOTTI, author of *A Storied Singer*

"In *Prevailing Winds,* Joseph Stanton's deep understanding of artists and their medium is everywhere evident in the ekphrastic poems of Section I, texts that go beyond the aesthetics of surfaces and invite us into a deeper narrative that brings the 'silent work of art' to life. In Sections II and III, his keen observations of the richness of wildlife in opposition to scenarios exploring the human condition are paintings in their own right and exemplify the incredible thematic range of Stanton's poetry."

—VALERIE ROBILLARD, author of *The Ekphrastic Moment in the Poetry of William Carlos Williams*

"The finely crafted *Prevailing Winds* collection by Joseph Stanton gathers within its pages three books: one on creation, another on inspiration—with ekphrastic and collaborative works—and one more on incarnation—recollections of intimacy with the mysterious divine through other people. All this is revealed through a rich repertoire of lyrical forms in a lush, paradisal setting."

—ERIC TINSAY VALLES, poet and director of Poetry Festival Singapore

"Many of us always eagerly await Joseph Stanton's next book, and here it is—and it won't disappoint. Once again, his poet's eye, in a fine frenzy rolling, fills the gap between imagination and reality, making of his local Hawaiian habitation a place of magic realism, beauty, and wisdom. A master of ekphrastic verse, Stanton continues that interest here, most notably in the series based on Winslow Homer's paintings and the collaborative poems produced for artist Adam LeBlanc's exhibit, *Nights on B Street. Prevailing Winds* is Stanton's best book yet."

—ROBERT HAMBLIN, author of *Myself and the World: A Biography of William Faulkner*

"Joseph Stanton's *Prevailing Winds* is a work of art. Indeed, the poems in its opening section, 'Representations," are about art: paintings and sculptures and installations, some whose makers he knows and with whom he has joined in collaborations, and others both past and present whose work he has pondered and loved. Visual art, like music, explores subjects and feelings that can't simply be expressed in words. But poetry, too, is an art. At its best, it becomes an almost magical new language within the language, using the same words, but choosing and ordering them in surprising ways, arranging their sounds so that they play with silence and evoke images and feelings more quickly than thought. An accomplished poet like Joseph Stanton, who has devoted his heart and mind lifelong to exploring the affinity between poetry and visual images, can 'raid the inarticulate' and find words to make the connections between the artist's feeling and our own, as he does in these poems. Other passionate subjects of this poet's attention include the natural world, especially as seen from or within the city. Trees, clouds, and especially birds engage him, both those surrounding him now—the finches, shamas, and frigate birds in 'Appearances'—and those native Hawaiian birds echoing from extinction, the honeycreepers and others in the section he calls 'Disappearances.' In a way, the final 'Disappearances' section has been set up for us by the last poem, 'Beached,' in the previous section, which hints that we're going to be asked to consider the extinction of more than species. The poems in this final section build on and resonate with one another. In several of them, Stanton considers the invisible man theme from various unique angles, and in others, such as 'Moth Monologues,' he explores the search for the meaning of disappearance in individual human death. This is not a collection of poems that could have been written by a young poet."

—SUE COWING, author of *Call Me Drog*

"The 'fragile poise' that is our stance in life despite knowing we will waste away and die is the theme of Joseph Stanton's *Prevailing Winds*. In his compressed narratives of humans, birds, and flowers, he describes the movement toward nothingness from the privileges of birth, health, and beauty. Yet wisdom and comfort can be found in these poems too."

—PAT MATSUEDA, author of *Bitter Angels*

"What distinct intelligence does the poet-critic bring to the beauty he inhabits, and the beauty that inhabits him? In Joseph Stanton's *Prevailing Winds*, we are invited to accompany the authority of the omniscient speaker as guide, as we walk through a triptych of rooms that in turn proffer representations, appearances, and disappearances. The view is sumptuous and sublime. In these poems remain lyric portraits of how art comes into being. Each poem offers a richly immersive space. The reader comes close to the page and language, to glean a choice fragment of history, identity, culture, tradition, authorship, process, textuality, all with great deliberate intent. Housed in this cool, clear voice is all the creative genius of such a staggering platter of preeminent artists. More importantly, through his calm intimations, we become witness to the conspicuous discernment of the eminent poet Stanton himself."

—DESMOND FRANCIS XAVIER KON ZHICHENG-MINGDÉ,
poet and founding editor of Squircle Line Press

# Prevailing Winds

poems by

## Joseph Stanton

SHANTI ARTS PUBLISHING
BRUNSWICK, MAINE

# Prevailing Winds

Published by Shanti Arts Publishing
Interior and cover design by Shanti Arts Designs

Cover image: Winslow Homer, *Hurricane,
Bahamas*. Watercolor and graphite on off-
white wove paper. 1898. Public domain.
Metropolitan Museum of Art, New York City.
www.metmuseum.org/art/collection/search/11124

Shanti Arts LLC
193 Hillside Road
Brunswick, Maine 04011
shantiarts.com

Printed in the United States of America

ISBN: 978-1-956056-37-2 (softcover)

Library of Congress Control Number: 2022936978

*for Barbara, Susan, and David*

# Contents

## DISAPPEARANCES

# REPRESENTATIONS

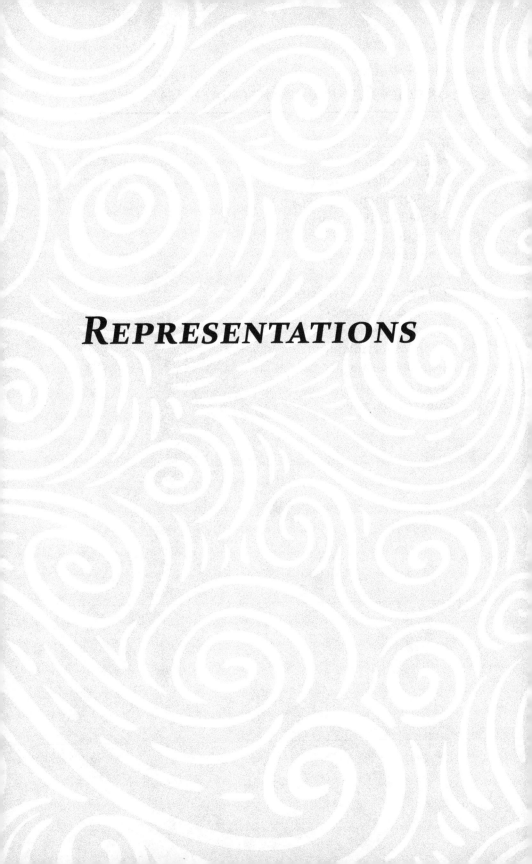

*Kloe Kang's*
## GARDEN ECLIPSE AT HOʻOMALUHIA

Bowls can rise to the sky
seeking to catch
in their hollowed hearts
long lost moons,
eclipsed in the garden
above the spectacle
of volcanic cliffs

and beyond whatever else can be
gathered and gilded
as rumors, as possibilities—
seedpods for holding,
bones for wishing,
shoes for dancing,
birds for dreaming.

*Kloe Kang's*
## BIRD OF PARADISE

A bird in these several hands,
dwells in a nest of gestures,
mudras enough for
an entire committee of bodhisattvas—
mudra of the touching of the ground,
mudra of the ubiquity,
mudra of the hiding of forms,
mudra of the absence of fear—

so that this bird in these hands
might be worth several more in the bushes,
gardens where geese
are beset by the sharp-toothed,
the predators of grounded eggs—
the cats, the rats, and that other goose,
the lithe and weaselly mongoose.

But this bird is played in these gestures
only as a bright beige card,
a lost dream of some other home—
not held, in any case, by these hands,
but remembered between them

and between their quiet commotions of gesture,
evocative of the flower
we call bird of paradise,
a blossoming that lacks
the true birds of its distant place.

In our pacific paradise
a bloom of this kind
can only be bred
by hands.

## Adam LeBlanc's
## *PREVAILING WINDS*

### Nowhere

Amidst my dings and arrows,
I am nested
between the dots and plots.

No one has trapped me
in these baubles of doubt,
these gleaming misdirections,

but I remain seated
because a chair
is there.

Of course, I know there is a sky,
but I linger inside myself,
wondering.

### Super Luminal Dithering

The background is plumb,
and I am descending,
losing face,
despite the bright device,
the books of pages turning
of their own accord,
arms moving,
octopi of an abstracted ocean.

When I reach the island,
I am surrounded by tweets,
but I search in vain
for the singing birds,
until I remember that snakes
have eaten them all.

Above me clouds
fill with memories,
without a drop
raining down.

## Whispering Shadow

A shadow floats inside me.
Faceless for now

it yearns to wear me like a mask.
It is the monster

I might have been
or might become.

In the dark, where none can see,
it is, even now, wounding the world.

I will strike a light
against it.

## After Damascus

An excess of light
knocks me down
on an ordinary road

and I think
I have been,

with joy and terror,
reborn.

But what comes after?

Stacking rock upon rock,
rock upon rock,
I will try to build
what might not fall.


## Glass Messengers

They come when least expected—
the angels, the devils.

I think I see right through them,
but, upon reflection,

I see that they
are me.


## Windy Day

A sparrow
is flying into the wind.
It cannot go forward,
will not fall back.

The wind, unrelenting,
a cold pastoral,
will not let it go,
but still it flies and flies,

caught in a brief eternity
of arrival.


## Prevailing Winds

In this thought
I walk the tall grasses
of the long lost place
we knew.

Sometimes I fight
a bitter breeze
as it breaks cold against me,
each step a struggle against
the whipping blades,
the snap of grasses across
my face.

Other times the wind is at my back,
parting the grasses,
and I am lifted with unexpected joy,
as if you were
just a step ahead,
dancing.


## Voyage

There is voyage and there is return.
Courage keeps to its boat of light

despite the maelstrom
and the many-headed monster.

Escape is unimaginable
and the only way to go.

## Adam LeBlanc's
## *NIGHTS ON B STREET*

### *The Grin in the Air*

Those nights on B Street
we all knew
to wear our own shoes,
to play our own hands.

Life or death
might be in the cards,
and the cards might be
up against some wall:

diamonds for what deludes,
hearts for all we've lost,
clubs for what might strike us,
spades for the final cost.

Sometimes we'd trust to luck,
sometimes we'd tempt fate,
but mostly it was just
one more night,

the air alive with sounds
or silences.
It was just a street to walk down,
just a place to hang out,

just a place to try to live,
hoping all would be all right
in the end
or in whatever might begin,

the moon a shining cat
against the fates in our stars,
that cat's grin disappearing behind clouds
or coming out again.

## Bounce

He bounces the ball
because it comes back.
When the playground clears,

he will shoot alone in the dark park,
out of doors but inside his mind,
where he battles

with only the distant streetlight
on his side,
at war with himself

over what he might be
or might not be,
throwing again and again

at an almost invisible goal
in a land of shadows.
The war goes on and on

and will not be lost
and will not be won.


## Blue Note

He plays for her, over and over,
"Never Let Me Go."
He feels the five notes
his pale sax sings,
never let me go,
a note for each sad syllable.

She is, he knows,
the tune, he plays,
blue on blue
notes that weep their song
because she is oh so very gone.
Only in his mind

does she sit on the stoop before
the closed red door.
The lateness of the night, too,
is a note he plays,
but absence is the why his sax sings,
his world, still yet, so full of her shadow.

Never let me go, he pleads
his breath floating the tune to the sky,
his sax whispering
to the moon's not-so-neon glow,
never
let me go.


## The Silhouettes

Some figures
on these streets
are only silhouettes,
figments of thoughts,
dreams lost

or not quite found,
that might have been
or once were,
ghosts of better
or ghosts of worse.


## The Last Shot

The shooter in black jacket
aims towards the pocket.
He shoots to win and can't afford to lose.
Everything, he thinks, rides on this.
The man sitting on the side,
the man in white, Mr. Bones,

is the devil in these details,
a conniver who can afford to lose,
but schemes to win.
A busty woman, a delectable shill,
steps towards the shooter.
She's in the employ of Mr. Bones

and tilts her distracting décolleté
towards the man in the black jacket.
Her job is to make him miss.
A waitress, also in league,
pretends to trip.
Her tray is about to crash to the floor.

Will that distraction turn the tide?
Or will black jacket prevail despite it all?
Red arrows of attention hang in air,
but the punchline is withheld.
Across the room two figures watch
but do not seem to care—

a man in blue leans back,
supported by nothing,
and a man in black
who wears a golden cap
bends forward, better to see
what happens next.

### The Waiting Woman

The woman at the window waits
for her man to find his way to her.
She frets because it's getting late.

He said he would be home by eight,
but now it's far beyond that hour.
The woman at the window waits

and thinks about his past mistakes
and listens for his car.
She frets because it's getting late.

She knows the pool hall is the bait,
the lure of bets and beer
The woman at the window waits

A winning night could change their fate,
but loss, she fears, is who they are.
She frets because it's getting late.

Because there is so much at stake,
he might go far too far.
The woman at the window waits
She frets because it's getting late.


## The Couple Outside the Bar

A woman in a red gown
and a man in a tuxedo embrace.
They do not care
that they are overdressed
for this neighborhood

and that their departure from the gala,
early and together,
would cause a fuss.
No one knows them on B Street
so they think this tryst anonymous,

a casual affair that will be
without consequence.
This, they think,
is just for fun,
but their story is the oldest one.

## At the Corner

The huckster sets up
his three-card-monte scam.
He thinks the bald man walking his dog
a likely mark.
A little boy is all eyes,
but his mother pulls him up the steps

Leaning down from the floor above,
the huckster's girl whispers,
"The coast is clear, no cops in sight."
The man with the dog
carefully fingers
the badge in his pocket.

Around the corner
the drummer, the guitarist,
and their sullen sister,
who might be induced to sing,
await what they hope
this night's foot traffic might bring.

At the corner an argument
finds a woman pointing left;
a man pointing right.
Their quarrel is a divide,
a righted angle,
a perpendicular.

She points towards home;
he towards one more bar.
They've reached
the end of a street,
a corner
for turning.

## The Smoker

This corner beneath the El gives him pause,
betwixt and between,
to stop for a smoke
in a zone of quiet, a moment of calm
within the riot of impossibilities
that is the city.

Even when the train roars overhead
this corner is a comfort.
All the rest hurry towards or hurry away
from the train.
Only this solitary smoker lingers
under the belly of the beast.

On this day
he has hotfooted here
his every step a burn of desire
for this private occasion
to consider an idea he is certain
will change his life.

Pocketed in this cool shadow
his mind is on fire
with all he will do,
all he will do.


## Outside the Studio

The sculptor, in splattered denim,
knows his art, as a cutting, a hollowing, a finding

of presence defined
by a surround of absence.

He hates that the dealer,
elegant in gray silk suit, fends off his gripe.

There was no contract the dealer explains;
he measures his words and clips them neatly.


## The Woman Dancing on the Roof

She is dancing
alone and for herself.
Her tight, white dress
swerves and curves and gleams
under the moon.

Her dancing plays
a tune against her life
and she twists the arrow of her song
down and around
whatever might come true.

## Chris Van Allsburg's
## *JUST DESERT*

What we prepare to open
can begin to glow under our hands
with an inner heart of light.

It is as if the wielded knife
sent ahead its bright wound.
This ripeness is a burning

without fire, a fever,
a passion to remain entire,
a desire never, ever to yield.

*Sandy Bleiffer's*

## PAPER SCULPTURES IN MEMORY OF WHAT HAPPENED IN HIROSHIMA ON 6 AUGUST 1945

Between here and back there is
a darkness full of no thing at all.

A torso of tumbled newsprint
has breasts in front, buttocks behind.

A melted window screen twists and turns,
refusing to wear its own shadow.

Legs gather in a far corner above
the brown, broken fragments of paper feet.

Burnt paper chests contain only absence—
standing dissemblances of skin.

The burning bush in the corner glows
green and mauve and fills with toes.

These parts can only dream of wholes.
Even a face can only be a façade.

A pair of pale legs touch sole to sole
and spread like a rumor of lost wings.

Fragments of charred angels molded from small
bodies try and try to climb the walls.

Autumnal leaves shaped as legs want
to find a way to walk into the sky.

## Jackson Pollock's
## PAINTING NUMBER 6

I spread the canvas on the floor and try to be at ease.
I walk around and around it, trying to be at ease.
I drip and drop slowly at first
and then quickly get quicker,
jumping around and around, dripping and dropping,
my arm slashing this way and slashing that,
never at rest.
I'm trying to get acquainted with what I'm doing.
Then, at last, I'm in the painting,
no longer aware of what I'm doing.
At last, I'm without fear.
I change and destroy, make and scrape and remake.

The painting speaks
and that speaking is me in motion,
the dance that is my making,
the spirit inside me is gone into an everywhere
that is paint, glass, and sand
on the canvas and on the floor.

I know when it is finished.
I give it a number.
It's the number that follows the one before.

*Isamu Noguchi's*
## THE STONE WITHIN

For Noguchi this carving into basalt
became a search for essence
beneath the skin—
a revelation so remarkable
that it could not be by chance.

Afterwards he felt compelled
to render the leftover fragments
into small finished pieces,
calling them
"the beautiful children."

## Isamu Noguchi's
## *BRILLIANCE*

Noguchi spoke basalt best of all.
It was his most intimate tongue,
harboring, as it did,
the double-ness
he so much loved.

In basalt he found a stone
that could be
dull skinned,
as red and rough
as the earth itself,

but with an interior
he could polish
to a gleam
of volcanic ink,
darkest of mirrors.

Basalt he knew as the core
of all erupted worlds—
even ocean floors,
even the moon and mars
hold basalt to heart.

In 1982 Noguchi
stacked three,
mismatched
chunks of basalt
as a column six-feet tall.

With diamond-edged saw
and diamond-tipped drill
he ripped
and broke
the igneous rock.

In some spots he polished
the inner revelation
to a blue-black sheen,
alternating rusted shell
and lava-liquid soul.

Then he wielded bamboo,
the most antique of tools
to pock a line
of marks
in ruddy skin.

When it was finished,
he called it *Brilliance*,
though he knew
it was less than that
and more.

## Isamu Noguchi's
### RED

A tall rectitude of red travertine,
one of Noguchi's monumental zeros,
full of nothing and nothing if not full,
speaks to his Euro mentor, Brancusi,
yet, also, seems as Zen as Zen could be,

wabi as well as sabi,
a statue that resides in a West that is also East,
Honolulu to be exact,
where Japan and America
cross in more ways than one,

a sculpture offering two sides,
an ancient rune whose tune
also declares the modern,
and we can see, too, that the smooth
is backed by the rough hewn,

balances struck and striking,

primitive, yet sophisticate,
powerful, yet simplistic,
rock that is also flesh,
containing crystals that spark light,
a sun setting on a Pacific expanse—

touching upon his mother and his father
as he often did in mind,
seeking, again,
the balance that is the everything
and the nothing at all.

## Francis Bacon's
### THREE STUDIES FOR A SELF PORTRAIT

A mirror, he feared,
could be full of tricks
so why not save face
by tripling it?
Bacon knew existence
questionable
so he never stopped questioning

what he himself
might be.
He loved to see in threes
with his triptychs
speaking to a holiness
of altered pieces.
Suggestive swerves

fleshed against absolute dark
constituting a reliquary:
an elusive self—
his own, for instance—
bespeaking a broken
remnant
of martyrdom.

*Edward Hopper's*
## SUMMERTIME

Hopper, the supposed Puritan, offers us here
a strawberry-blond almost-nude;
her thin blue-white dress
hiding next to nothing.

Because the pale hue
of her frock echoes the gray-blue
of discretely concrete architecture
in summer light,
everything on view
seems, at first to sing
a monochrome of stone,
a cool harmony of calm,
but there burns
at the heart of the scene
a passionate aria,
a covertly revealed blond body
(really Jo's figure in disguise),
bra-less breast glowing
through a painterly
pretense of linen.

The building's door,
gaping wide behind her,
offers another sort
of warmth of tone—
as sensuous in its own way as the woman—
the red-brown wood of its opened frame
whispering
a vaginal dark.

## George Ault's
## LAST PAINTING OF RUSSELL'S CORNERS

He loved the lamp that made the corner bright,
adored it as a stay against the dark,
but dark returned when he moved past the light.

The chaos of his era out of sight,
his deft Precision kept his vision stark,
shaped by the lamp that made the corner bright.

Against the tumult of the world he posed this site;
he dreamt geometry as if a truth were clear,
but dark returned when he moved past the light.

This Catskill village was his whole delight,
his universe had Woodstock at its heart,
a tiny town had made his corner bright.

He painted roofs to shoulder up the night,
and walked this road, avoiding shadowed forks,
but dark returned when he moved past the light.

Beyond himself in art, he could not quite
decide to live and plunged into the dark.
He loved the lamp that made the corner bright,
but dark returned when he moved past the light.

*Winslow Homer's*
# THE SHARPSHOOTER ON PICKET DUTY

Homer knew the horror
of a war not at all civil
that marked the start
of modern war unfair.

A captain once described
the job of sharpshooting
as only to "watch and kill."

Stationed in tall pines,
a sharper's sight telescopic
could kill from one mile away.

Sometimes a soldier,
gathering firewood,
abruptly fell dead.

"With everything as silent as the grave
here would come one of those rifled balls
and cut a hole clear through you."

## Winslow Homer's
# HOME, SWEET HOME

Irony's at home here.
Ever so humble, indeed,
are the tiny tents of residence,
where a pair of soldiers sadly listen,
to a regimental band,

discernible in the distance,
playing the most popular of songs.

The soldiers' thoughts
wish away the war,
as they hear and re-hear
the bitter sugar sweet
chorus sound and repeat.

There's no place like home.
There's no place like home.

## Winslow Homer's
## CROQUET SCENE

After the Civil War
Winslow turned toward
a different sort of war,
a newly imported game women
could play as well as men.

Some claim women
played it much better than men.

And Homer, who loved women,
made a trio of lovely females his stars—
each gal a spectacular triangle of fabric
topped with a determined face.

Their faces for the game,
their "game faces" we might say,
declaring a desire to win the day,
despite the hampering
splendors of expansive gowns.

In *Croquet Scene,*
the best known of the five paintings,
one man, who seems to be
Winslow his very self
is down on one knee
before a determined woman in red attire.

Here's the joke:
his obeisance mimics
what could appear to be
a proposal to the lady in crimson,
but, in fact, he is merely
posing the ball of her opponent.
in a fatal position.

The woman in red is about
to clobber the ball
of the woman in blue,
to "croquet" it,
to knock it viciously away
towards the distant trees.

Homer, whose face we cannot see,
is represented only by the top of his straw hat,
which declares him a mere zero
as he bends before
these gloriously gorgeous warriors,

who seem oblivious to their own
all conquering beauty,
wanting only, at this moment,
to slap a wooden ball
victoriously
through a metal hoop.

*Winslow Homer's*

# ARTISTS SKETCHING IN THE WHITE MOUNTAINS

Landscape artists must be, we know,
part of the landscapes they see.
Homer's wry joke here gives us a row
of daubers in the midst of White Mountains—

each nattily dressed
but not at all picturesque
or sublime—
intrusions on the scene

with easels, palettes, and umbrellas—
unlovely against a lovely horizon
of clouds, mountains, and flowers.
The last of these sketchers

is Winslow himself—
his characteristic mustache
apparent and his name signed
on the backpack behind him.

That this is an occasion
for painterly camaraderie
as much as artistic productivity
is evident on the far left

where a bottle of wine
nests in a stump cleft,
cool and waiting
for the sun's set.

## *Winslow Homer's*
## *BRIDLE PATH, WHITE MOUNTAINS*

Back from Paris, Homer chose a new path.
A woman riding high in White Mountains
becomes his largest canvas,
and a place to pose a newly special friend.

He sketched a tourist on the trail. In studio,
his model is Helena on a chair.
On canvas he lends her a special glow.
She is for him the fairest of the fair.

She likes Winslow and loves his wit
and knows he sets her on this trail to star
in a tenderly affectionate drift
of thought: a bridal plan, that is, far

from what she wants from her master in art.
She know this rocky ride may break his heart.

*Winslow Homer 's*

## A SUMMER NIGHT

The two women are dancing in the moonlight,
twirling in between the glow of the house
and the gleam of the moon breaking on the sea—

turning and turning on the worn planking
of the porch that faces the rocky shore
where friends have gathered themselves
into piles of silhouettes

shored up against
the play of light whitening
the robin's-egg-blue sea
between grim gesturings of black rock.

This one's dreaming smile reminds him of Helena,
and he suddenly sees
he must capture the wave spuming behind her.

*Winslow Homer's*
# HURRICANE, BAHAMAS

The buildings crouch before the storm,
but palm trees hold vertical
against the sheen of wind-driven sky,
each treetop an anxious asterisk of green.

Winslow loved coco palms.
His strokes of brush
define how pinnate leaves
curve to withstand a blast.

A slice of blue blue sea,
glimpsed at foreground left,
suggests the whipping wind
is not the story's end.

## Thomas Cole's
## *EXPULSION FROM THE GARDEN OF EDEN*

Cole's *Expulsion* tries in part of its heart
to be about Eden as well as its aftermath.
In Eden, on the right (of course)
the grass is, necessarily, greener;

the deciduous trees feather
a gentleness suggestive
of extenuating circumstances,
an oxygenation of light

that pales the greens at the tips
of most leaves and speaks
of the tenderness of Heaven
for unfallen pairs—the deer frolicking,

the swans serenely floating—
but the pair Cole wants to care about—
trudging Eve and lamenting Adam—
are paying the price for their bites

of the fruit of knowledge—
expelled, exit stage left, a fated fall,
a sudden hypothesis-testing
that ended their bliss.

It would almost seem, though,
that Eden wants them back
so fondly does the rainbow tumble
of flowers extend towards them

fingers of color reaching beyond
the judgmental fall of rock wall
and harshly lighted gash of gateway.
But the creeping carpet of thwarted

affection cannot soften the explosion
of angry, golden light that propels
our first parents from the jagged gate.
God's anger here has many symptoms,

but Cole does without the sword and slash
of Renaissance archangel.
Here divinity speaks only au natural.
Beyond the violent radiance of expulsion

a volcano erupts, a waterfall tumbles,
a Turneresque vortex of cloud twirls.
But all here is not without hope.
At bottom, beneath the blasted trees,

the true citizens of American wilderness—
a stalking wolf and a ravenous vulture
watch and wait
in hopes of a revivifying meal.

# APPEARANCES

# FINCHES ROILING AT SUNSET

Some sunsets feature clouds of tiny birds soaring
in patterns shifting, roiling against the orange
like nothing we can understand,
an ungraspable swirling geometry

of air and light populated by tiny specks
that lift by the hundreds from trees
to circle and re-circle to almost land in other trees
and then to ascend again spinning

a feathered fabric inexplicable
and seen, it would seem, only by me,
though all around me crowds of people hurry
spinning to their inner gyres,

earthbound echoes
of what the finches do more beautifully.

# FINCHES AT DUSK IN THE TREETOPS

I love these drum-brush flutterings,
this crescendo of tiny, piping songs
I already hear as I climb
the stairs to find them.
I am rising
to the roof at dusk
to a kingdom of wings,
finches converging from all sides,
roosting in the treetops,
some re-circling again and again
as they jockey for perches,
a game of very musical chairs.

I stand motionless on my rooftop
and let their excited diving flights
whiz around me,
as if I were just
a tree trunk or a rock,
some bullet past, inches from my ear,
sweet whispers of wind.

Most dusks I estimate
200 waxbills,
50 chestnut mannikins,
and our precious shama thrush,
lifting its gorgeous, lilting song.

I speak of the splendor
of these massive featherings
to anyone who will listen.

But a friend rails
angrily against them,
"If I stand in the bamboo,"
he snarls,
"shit rains down on my head."

"Then don't," I solemnly advise,
"stand in the bamboo."

# FRIGATE BIRD

Hale'iwa'o namo declares it,
the hale of the 'iwa, the house of the frigate bird.

Most days you can spy one of those big-winged, fork-tailed rascals
soaring overhead
in flight no plane or kite could match,
cruising fast lanes of upper air,
soaring effortlessly for hours,
then, with a slight shrug of shoulder and tilt of tail,

accelerating a long, down-wind dive,
wings brandishing their swords
for a rapid descent
aimed at the head of a smaller bird,
startling it into spitting up its meal,
which the 'iwa snatches mid-air.

Elegance of form is like that sometimes—
just a way to steal somebody's lunch.

# ALBATROSS

They are so wide of wing—
a seven-pound bird has a seven-foot wingspan—
that they can glide high in the sky

without flapping;
or just above the waves,
seeking squid for eating.

When they land on land they crash,
stumbling into bushes to break their fall.
Goony birds observers have called them.

But when they mate
they dance and dance and dance,
then go back to soaring.

# KULA SKYLARK

—for Ali'i Chang

This bird, thatched to be unseen in grass,
scampers in Kula's purpling rows of lavender,
searching for bugs and bits of seed.
It could be nothing more than an odd sparrow
sporting a flash of white at tail
for all we know or care, as we picnic in cool air,
steeped in last light and flowers.

But, when the skylark rises to its song,
singing up and up
till it's almost out of sight,
a tiny dot chiming sharp, bell tones
towards a sweetly strange, elaborated crescendo
that can be heard for miles in the open air,
our minds will fill with a rapture of lark.

Shelley's blithe spirit whistles for us
high in the suddenly pink sky of this Pacific place—
while the ocean shimmers below,
beyond the coming lights of Lahaina.
Singing for us the skylark seems to be,
as Shakespeare was inspired to say on another island,
hymns at heaven's gate.

# DRIVING HOME TOGETHER ON VALENTINE'S DAY

I point out to her
something I have noticed
over the long years
of this long commute:

only the larger birds—
mynahs, egrets, herons—
dare the scary flight
over the highway

during rush hour traffic.
I especially love to see
the mynahs who mostly
fly across as pairs,

mates flapping in tandem,
sometimes their wings
almost touching,
inseparable,

despite the squawking
mynah household squabbles
we see on the sidewalks.
We are riding the rush hour

for yet another
Valentine's Day—
me talking, she sleeping—
almost touching.

# SAFFRON FINCHES

A path winds the coast of the Harbor.
We hike a marsh, a farm, a refuge for birds,
and then the odorous bulk of a power plant.

We see the wildlife we expected—
stilts, moorhens, herons, mynahs, egrets—
but then there is that one surprise,

saffron finches suddenly everywhere,
little fellows bursting lemony light
in the air in front of us and behind.

All that bright yellow, yellow, yellow
made the day lighter, and, in the bushes,
all those little pockets of saffron, singing.

# SINGING WITH THE SHAMA

Outside my window a shama thrush,
most melodious of Oʻahu singers,
gurgles his liquid tunes as he cavorts

in the spray of the sprinkler in my garden.
He frequents that sprinkler
despite my presence a few feet away,

in my shower, singing, too.
Sometimes, though, as I croon,
"500 miles, 500 miles..."

he stops his warble mid note,
as if to declare he does not do duets.

# THE BAOBAB TREE AT THE ART BUILDING

A tree that can grow
for centuries rises
beside us,

an enormity unremarked
as we come and go,
killing time.

# BLUE MARBLE TREE

Pure blue, rare in the natural world,
falls all around us here.
This tree drops perfectly round marbles
so blue that, when I first saw them,
I thought them a hoax
or an accidental tossing
of blue plastic toys.

But no these are
what the tree makes.

Hindus tell two tales:
in one they call each blue fruit
a tear Shiva shed in compassion
for the miseries of the world;
in the other Shiva is weeping
blue in midst of battle against Tripura,
the cities of demonic Asuras.

Take your choice:
the blue of pity or the blue of war.

Either way we all
get the blues sometimes
and these can become—
when the fruit rots away—
rudraksha beads, symbolic, the Hindus say,
of souls that are lost
but in sight of God.

# SAGA TREE

Color comes to us
from everywhere here.
Across from our blue marble tree
a huge saga tree
scatters blood
in the grass at our feet.

A woman cried and cried
for her man never returned from war.
When her tears ran dry she wept drops of blood.
From this grief, they say in Singapore,
came the bright red seeds
of the saga tree.

These beads are believed to be
bearers of luck.
Hollow a drop of scarlet
and fill it with elephants
and you will have one wish fulfilled
for every elephant inside.

Before the practice was banned
seeds were sold containing
100 tiny tiny elephants
that children went blind carving.
Such is the price
of good fortune.

# THE TREE OF LIFE

A breadfruit tree is a staff of living,
its shapely leaves
beloved by makers of Hawaiian quilts,

and its balled fruits
bakeable to a fibrous bread—
a delight, sometimes, when we do it right.

In ancient times
Hawaiians smeared the tree's sticky gum
thickly on its branches,

making traps of tenderness
for beautiful birds,
plucking a few bright feathers

from each,
then washing
and releasing the birds back to the sky.

# EAR POD TREE

Once a year:
the tallest tree on my path
drops large brown ears
on the road, in the grass.

Everywhere
I look are these
strange, gleaming vestiges
of gigantic heads.

Sometimes I collect them
on my window sill.

They rest there,
beauties gorgeous
and all aglow
but unknowable.

No matter what I say to them,
no matter with what urgency
or passion I speak to them,
they never listen to me,

even though
they are all ears.

# Hala

The pandanus,
the oldest of God plants—
sporting aerial roots
as evidence of transcendence—

came to these islands
long before our world
of freeways, hotels,
and shopping malls—

the screwpine
twisted into the heart of things.

A Hawaiian tale claims
humankind arrived
when a god cut her finger and bled
while weaving the sharp, serrated hala leaves:

one drop the woman,
one drop the man—

from this the trouble came.

# SANDALWOOD

Hiking the Wai'anae, we're surprised
to see a sandalwood tree,
ancient remnant
miraculously in bloom, high

in mountain air
secured by roots—
insidious, parasitic—
adhering to an obscure crag.

Blossoming bright red,
it drops remembrances
of trails past
where the long-ago men—

bent question marks—
stumbled, bleeding,
under aromatic burdens
of broken heartwood,

bringing down
to the greedy kings and merchants
the sweet, precious (now forgotten)
fragrance.

# WHITE GINGER

Picked ginger, a glory of fragility, perfumes,
ever so briefly, a person or a room.

There are those who avoid the odor,
but for me it's a sudden door—

discovered sometimes
on the edges of my lawn—

that opens to the sky
what the ground might be

or the other way
around.

# CLOUDS AGAINST CLIFFS

Tourist brochures gaze
mostly out to sea,
claiming for Hawai'i
a kind of scenic
that is only
endless beach,

but, for many of us,
mauka is what we like to see—
the bright, falsetto clouds
singing against the rock-ribbed,
slack-key rhythms
of the soaring cliffs.

# THE KOʻOLAUS AFTER A STORM

The torrential downpour
gives up its ghosts.

Clouds broken into
whispers of feathery white
drift slowly across green ridges
rife
with waterfalls.

In sudden sunlight we face
more rainbows
than we
could possibly need.

# AT COFFEE MĀNOA, CLOUDS RISING

Dark French roast,
the steam rising and drifting
from the white cup
with the green picture
of the volcanic cliffs
that rise green before me,
as I sit drinking and looking.

Some days it's so quiet
it's as if everyone
has been gone
a long, long time.

Clouds whiter than the cup
rise and drift.
Dark birds draw lines of flight
against the cliffs, rising
above the parked cars, the trees
bright green in the bright
late-afternoon light.

I am watching
the cliffs on the cup,
the white clouds rising.

# BEACHED

Everywhere we look
where the sea presents itself
we think of sand

as ground to stand on,
a place to play.
There is no need,

most of the time,
to try to comprehend
its shifting drifts,

its myriad mausoleum,
its ocean-gathered remnants,
all those tiny bones.

# DISAPPEARANCES

# EYES

Eyes might be
mirrors,
reflecting only sky.

But we float behind,
clouds that think
they are thinking.

We are not hiding.
We are just behind,
lagging,
seeking to know.

If you were to look,
you might find me.
If I were to look,
I might find you.

We are attempting
to understand,
failing mostly, but trying,
really trying.

As I turn to you
to share my thoughts,
I look into your eyes,
you look into mine.

# A MAN MELTED ON MAUNAKEA STREET TODAY

It all starts innocently enough:
under the shadow of the Cultural Plaza
a shoe protrudes from a battered can—
the brown leather scarred and cracked,
the undone laces spilling out
like rhododendrons
or blood.
Not a pretty sight
but hardly evidence of foul play.

Then, a block makai,
there appears
down the alley toward
C. Q. Yee Hop & Co.
a pair of socks twisted
in an agony of nylon,
suspicious-looking holes at toes.

Meanwhile, at Pauahi Street,
a pair of pants is caught in midstride
crossing the intersection,
broken at the knees
by traffic of the ordinary day.

By the time I reach Hotel Street
I am ready for that one solitary sleeve,
waving,
a sad, unlaundered pleading
in the breeze whipping between
indifferent office buildings.

Beyond King Street's
desperate canyon
a blue-paisley tie

tries to slither through a chain-link fence,
but there is no way out.
A MAN MELTED ON MAUNAKEA STREET TODAY.
the thought hits like a glimpsed headline,
an apotheosis
or a routine demise
in the naked city
where thousands of stories unravel
or climb skyward.

High above Honolulu Harbor
floats a hat that's lost its head
or a wadded newspaper.
I can't tell at this distance.
It's just a dot behind a line of clouds.

# MOTH MONOLOGUES

*"In Hawai'i, the Black Witch Moth is thought to be
the soul of a dead person coming back to say goodbye."*

1

Giant son,
you weighed upon us
always heavier and heavier.

In childhood you were round,
but, then, become a man,
you kept rounding out and out.
What could we do?

Food was beside the point.
Even when you ate little
obesity became you.

And now the heavy weather
of your soul floats you back to us,
a light flutter of dark in the eaves.


2

Husband, you complained
I did not love you,
but all I wanted
was a home for our child,
a hope for our future.

So I begged and begged you:
get a better job,
earn more money.
Was I wrong in that?
Was I wrong to ask for a decent life?

Did you think crashing
your car at 100mph
late that night
would solve anything
for me? for our child?

And now you
come on powdered wings
pleading in your weak way,
as if I could forgive you,
as if I could ever have loved you.


3

Sister,
we shared a childhood,
but damaged of mind as you were,
I never knew you.

The best
was when you managed
to smile and mumble "little brother"
while I read to you.

I feared the rages
that made you
bang your hand against your head
or your head against the wall.

And now you pound black wings
against our picture window,
and I fear you
again.

4

Brother, brother, we miss you so.
We hated—oh, how we hated that war—
and that you had to go,

and now you have come back so very far
and have no way to know
that you can only beat against the door.


5

Father, in your last years
you lived only to run the car
you could no longer drive.

You hobbled out to the driveway
late at night in all weathers,
to gun the battery

you obsessively feared would die.
Now it is you who have died,
and yet still we hear you

still trying to come back,
whispering against the window,
wanting back in

after yet another
stumble
in the desperate dark.


6

Friend, when we barred together
inside the neon night
the juke primed songs
younger than we were young,

the plink of balls in pockets
punctuated
what we had to say concerning
the pure products of our Smith Coronas.

Now, when I drink alone,
the songs sound bluer
and over supplied with absence,
and the green fields of felt are gone

and plinks now light tiny screens
to which the drinkers bow,
while outside in absolute dark
a thought of you rises,

beating against the glass,
in search of the olden neon—
the lost alphabets of red and blue,
the lost numbers of orange and green.


7

Mother,
so sad you were to leave me.

You feared I could not do without you,
child that I still was.

In the last days,
you tried to smile through the cancerous pain,

but the grimace had to come
flickering across your frightened face.

And now, well past your death,
you have come to see how I have fared.

Rest, my dear, your beating wings.
I could be better, but I could be worse.

# QUESTIONS FOR DAD

Last night I came to my father
to query him:

What had happened to our house?
And to my corner bedroom
with its one window towards the backyard,
where my dog was barking
at the approach of dawn
and its other window
towards the Meztgar's driveway,
where their delinquent son
was whistling between puffs on his cigarette?

And where was my mother
and my sister Kathy?
He could not answer,
I remembered abruptly,
because he had been dead
for fifty years.

But somehow the questions still lingered
for a few precious seconds,
hanging in the air between us,
as I faced him waiting
at the foot of his bed
as he propped himself up on one elbow
and seemed to be thinking about it all
with me still waiting and waiting,
for some insane reason,
so momentarily sure
he would answer.

# *Asbestos*

Fibers from the gods, miraculous
metallic wool gathered in secret clefts
of metamorphic rock. Cure for all ills
the ancients believed this downy fluff
from rock. Pliny the Elder wrote of shrouds
that would not burn, would not be consumed.
An airy iron so perfect it seemed absurd
and was.
        Motes of dust dance round the room
in shafts of light they spin and fall and rise
as doors open to workers walking through.
Dust unto dust returns, soft as sighs.
I have worked in such a room and so have you.

# TO MY INSOMNIA

What is it you want from me?
Each night there is less left to take,
but you keep digging for more and more

as if you would leave me hollowed,
the shell of my life moving feebly
through its stark absence of dreaming,

moving forward still but cautioned
by a fragile poise any breeze
could suddenly shatter.

# "WARNING: DOOR IS ALARMED"

In the post-op days of my hospital stay
they help me shuffle down the corridors
to restore some of what has gone away—
my natural knacks, my bodily mechanics.
I seem an absurdly hobbled version of myself,
exuding more tubing than a VCR.

To be fully alive again seems unlikely—
a goal elusive, mocking, ever out of reach,
like a door at the far end of a hall
that I creep towards for what seems like decades,
as it recedes, taking with it its anxious message:
that it is alarmed, that it is ready to scream.

"Yeah," I tell the door when I finally get there,
"me, too."

# THE WEB OF AN ORB WEAVER

In this woven orb an ending waits.
Who knew a life could have such symmetry?
A mosquito, a moth, a tiger swallowtail—
each flies a random path it thinks,
pursuing food, or sex, or sunlight

until stopped of a sudden in silk.
What could this be? we say
when a pain at heart or a cough
comes sudden and unannounced.
An ending might be a veil

beautiful beyond belief
suspended in some Eden's garden
in front of a sunlit brightness
we want, oh so very desperately,
to reach.

# YORICK REPLIES TO HAMLET

You pity me, my callow prince,
young as you are and melancholy?
I lived for jokes, as you well know,
one joyous gibe after another,
but being dead is not as bad
as thinking of it, and yet
this grimmest of consummations
is never sincerely wished for,
even by you, despite your pale
and whining fatalistic
grumblings, devout or otherwise.

Listen to me, Hamlet, sage advice
from my skull to yours; the dead king lies.
The only poison in the ear
is his words in yours. Your uncle
loved your mother, it is true;
but so did many others.
Even I might be your father.
Who could blame her? The king
loved only soldiery
and beardless soldiers; that's why he
comes now crying to you, young man,
to bring him his consolation.
He wants to see the blood flow, hot and red,
and you, fair prince, will be among the dead.

If you could hear my ghosted voice
over the sad clamor of your mind,
I could save you yet, but the stars
have scripted an ill-fortuned end.

One last bone I have for you
of my gravest common sense,
a parting word to the wise enough
to stay alive: all skulls smile
and all ghosts lie. The rest is silence.

# THE ISMS OF DORIAN GRAY

Dorian Gray, Pointillist
> With a gasp
> it seemed he was not,
> but he was, at long last,
> a dot.

Dorian Gray, Cubist
> At the end his assets
> shifted their facets.

Dorian Gray Surrealist
> There was
> a final scream,
> and then he was
> his dream.

Dorian Gray, Abstract Expressionist
> When he died with a shriek
> he was, suddenly,
> a lavender streak.

Dorian Gray, Pop Artist
> At the last he turned pale
> and became a can of ale.

# THE WALKER-THROUGH WALLS

*after a tale by Marcel Aymé*

The about-to-be-captured thief found that
re-doubled concentration
could enable him to walk through walls.

Unexpectedly trapped in a vault
his deepest mind surged to realign his molecules
as he pressed, in desperation, against the cold steel,

and, suddenly, there he was,
out on the sidewalk
with the sun bright and a breeze blowing,

but, overjoyed at the turn the day had taken,
the thief trusted
his trick too much.

The next night,
while attempting entry into a jewelry store,
lustful musings about a woman he had just seen

caused his focus to slip,
and there he was, with profound chagrin,
stuck forever in brick.

# THE AUTOMATIC DECAY
## OF ANDRÉ BRETON'S CORPSE

The exquisite corpse shall drink the new wine.
The exquisite corpse shall drink the new
The exquisite corpse shall drink the
The exquisite corpse shall drink
The exquisite corpse shall
The exquisite corpse
The exquisite
The

# Variations on a Theme by Franz Kafka

### 1

He didn't know who they represented
or what charges they had to bring against him,
but he knew there would be forms to sign
and important, inaccessible people
he would need to see.
But did he guess he would be shot down,
like a dog,
for writing his name on the wrong line?

### 2

As an alien who had come
from a ghetto to survey a new land,
he knew there would be a castle
where he would try to register
his existence.
Yet he feared the entrances
might all be exits
or that the lines might be infinite corkscrews
that turn on themselves
without ever opening anything.
He tried to get ahead by seducing a stenographer,
shifting her carriage and tangling her ribbon,
but she declared she couldn't help him
because he didn't have the correct form.

3

At first, the startling discovery
that he had dream created himself
into a cockroach did not worry him.
Quickly learning to love the flavor
of his decayed humanity
he made his room a cozy womb
of rotting furniture.
He chuckled, wiggling his antennae,
when he discovered
walls made better floors.
At night he indulged
in an ecstasy of scampering.
But in the morning
he was canceled like a postage stamp
and tossed into the circular file
for dead letters,
because he did not fit
into any of the approved
classifications.

# After Reading Kerouac

He showed us how to understand
the shy, secret shine of words
like *holy* and *sweet* and *sad;*

how to witness them without apparent concern,
floating, lovely, in their little clouds
of demure semantic glory;

how to see them close at hand,
while knowing our holy bodies are rotting
and our sweet, beloved mothers' bodies are rotting,

and it's all so insanely sad.
In that sad, sweet, and holy way he had
in some lost, late-afternoon,

just-before-neon-evening,
long-shadowed-jazzy musing,
he could let the biggest questions

break against
his rocky, tender heart
like the night-sized waves at Big Sur.

Now that he's free
of the slaving meat wheel
and safe in heaven dead

who *is* ever going to know
the wobbling world
before it goes?

# YOU'RE RIGHT, WE'RE LEFT, HE'S GONE

We are blue and the shoes are, too,
but we will lay offa those.
A song tells us to,
a song that tells us the shoes were suede,
and we can see they danced

the grief his moves put him through,
as he swiveled and swayed,
and now we're left,
knowing he was right
to try to get real down,

though he was led astray anyway by his rise
into one bad flick after another,
one shoe on the right,
the other shoe on the left,
(with those hips swiveling above,

transcendent, maybe),
a pair if we ever saw one,
like the shoes Van Gogh painted,
knowing he had no chance,
but wanting to dance.

# FOR SINATRA IN THE WEE SMALL HOURS

Look at yourself, you voice, so very glad
to be unhappy, though unrequited love's
a bore, and you've got it pretty bad,

and you can't get along without her,
no, not really very well, though you try
and try to be so glad to be unhappy

and smile long notes through a mood indigo,
your blues so cool, holding the smiling whiskey
of your aging vibrato, swirled in the glass

of unrelenting style, deep in a dream
of some sort of her we've all lost, too, with you
seeing all our losses, as if you were singing

somehow all our sorrows, every life we've
wept tearless in the wee small hours, mourning
with a smile and a last, long curl of smoke,     adrift.

# Ways of Disappearing

With pursuers almost on your heels
duck into an alley,
recompose yourself,
and join the pursuit—
exclaiming,
"Where could he have gone?"

Be an actor
pointing at the moon
so beautifully
that the audience sees
only the moon.

Happen
not to live
forever.

# NOW YOU SEE HER

In the classic magic trick prisms
reflect light around an object
so that the thing cannot be seen.

Thus a cat can be made to disappear
into a picture, leaving behind
only its meow.

But movies do disappearance best:
a long line of people can be made
to disappear into the side of a tree.

It's like what happens to everyone
you knew in childhood
if you live long enough.

# RECIPE FOR INVISIBILITY FROM
# A BOOK ON WITCHCRAFT

Into well water poured into a black pot
at the stroke of midnight,
place the bones of a black cat.

Boil them for 24 hours.
hold one of the bones
in your hand and say,
"Accept my offering and don't delay."

Try each bone in turn
until you cannot see your face
reflected in the water.

Keep that bone for future use.

# REGRETS OF THE INVISIBLE MAN

He's always
counted absent.
No amount of raising his hand
lets him ask a question
or summon a taxi.
Haircuts and
dental work
can only be hit or miss.
Chairs are safe for him
only in
empty rooms.
He can see beautiful women in dishabille,
but, when he winks and whistles,
they turn to the teapot.

# DEATH OF THE INVISIBLE MAN

Disdaining the crosswalk
he darts across the middle of the block
and is run over by a truck.
The driver, of course, saw nothing.
The invisible man
remains an unseen
bump in the road for months.

# PHILODORIA

So much depends upon a rare bug
as tiny as a single eyelash,
a micromoth on Moloka'i

radiated from its ancestor
millions and millions
of years before homo sapiens

even dreamed of arriving,
a micromoth
that lives for and in

a plant, also rare,
that needs the moth, too.
For lack of one or the other

a forest might be lost
or might
never have been.

# HONEYCREEPERS

## Prologue

Honeycreepers speciated,
theory has it,
from an irruption of rose finches
wind-driven to these islands
four-million years ago,
give or take a million years.

Entrapment on an island
changes body and soul
all of us know
who live on these
rocks in the sea.

From pairs of adamic finches
these divergent multifoliates rose,
and rise still,
but extinction's grim harvester
hunts them,
his sickle sighing in the breeze.

## I'i'wi

This flash of red,
pure of pigment
hovers hummingbird-like
in front of a flower,
which is its twin in color,
red on red in mid-air.
This bird's beak is curved
for drinking deep
of the deeply curved cups
that hold 'ōhi'a nectar.

Because the 'ōhi'a lives high
in the highest peaks
a colony of i'i'wi can linger
up there accidentally
above the fatality
that is the mosquito disease—
every year fewer of these
flickers of scarlet
rise to their occasions.

## 'Apapane

When the 'ōhi'a blossom count is high
'apapane, the red bird
most sacred to the Hawaiians,
formerly was almost easy to find
on all islands, even O'ahu.

While the female nests,
the male continuously,
defiantly sings out—
sometimes a whistle,
sometimes a chirp—

saying, maybe,
"we are making
another of her, another of me."

## 'Akepa

The tiniest of the creepers,
they boast the brightest orange
of any bird in the world.

To breed they need
the tops of high trees
and the right-sized pukas.

Rarer and rarer every year,
they can still sometimes be seen
high in the tallest of koa trees—

tiny orange balls
bouncing in beams
of last light.

## ʻAkiapolaʻau

Peck, peck, peck
it goes with its lower beak,
breaking wood to reveal bugs
for its curved upper beak
to dig out.

The Hawaiian woodpecker
some call it
because its tap, tap, tapping
reverberates in the woods
until its singing takes over.

"Cheedle-ee"
it warbles sometimes.
"Sweet!" it says, too,
when warranted.

## Kiwikiu

This bird,
yellow trimmed with green,

we call a parrot bill
for its parrot-hammer beak

that lets it crack branches,
opening them for sweetmeat grubs.

The few hundred kiwikiu
lingering on the steep slopes

of Haleakalā
sing "cheer-up, cheer-up"

without really meaning it.


## ʻAkohekohe

A blackish bird
thatched with white and gold
and a flashy fluff of feathers
above it its beak

that makes it seem the Elvis
of the creepers.

The biggest of these birds,
it bullies the rest—

telling the iʻiʻwi and the ʻapapane
to get out of its ʻōhiʻa lehua
by sundown.


## ʻŌʻū

Bright yellow of head,
dark green of body,
these bigger honeycreepers
could fly far and wide on their strong wings,

up slope and down slope,
for fruit and buds and bugs.

But their strength was their undoing,
with down-slope ventures
putting them in the path
of malarial mosquitos.
The 'ō'ū's song, too, went up and down,
a sweet sweet canary tune
we now can never hear
this just-now-extinct bird sing.


## 'Akialoa

The curved bill,
almost as long as the rest of his body,
of this extinct

brown-backed, yellow-bellied creeper,
helped it probe crevices for bugs
and seek the deep, sweet nectar of lobelias.

European collectors of carcasses and feathers
noted the strong bonds of mated 'akialoas.
When they shot one of a pair,

the other would repeatedly return
searching for its mate,
until it, too, could be collected.

In many cases the last of a species
was shot and mounted by a scientist
who passionately loved the bird,
sought it tirelessly,
and rejoiced in having been able,
at last,
to collect it.

# THE LAST KAUA'I 'Ō'Ō

In 1983, in the highest branch of a tree
in a deeply forested place
a male 'ō'ō called and called to his mate—

ringing tones echoing, echoing—
far and far, a quarter-mile at least
his yearning bell tolling

the remains of wild Kaua'i.
In the pauses between the calling,
he was gathering,

building the nest his mate would need,
building it stronger, building it better,
building towards her return.

At least once every year
he was seen to try his song—
his cry eerie, penetrating.

In 1987, his song soared one last time
and then arrived the silence,
and he was known to be, at last,
the last of his kind.

# THE NIGHT OF THE 'A'O

Young shearwaters fledge on clear nights,
flying off their nested places of birth,
seeking the brightest part of the sky.

In olden days that would aim them
towards moon and stars,
astronautical ambition leading them always offshore

to commence careers feeding on high seas.
But now our night-time electrifications
sometimes confuse their flights

so that fledge-night birds descend
on backyards, on shopping malls,
on all our lighted night places.

Some autumn nights flocks of shearwaters
rain down suddenly
on a high school football game,

making it seem a scene by Hitchcock,
the horror mostly in the hearts of the birds
who cannot lift off from level ground

and need to be,
by the kindness of strangers,
carried to the sea.

# ARTWORK REFERENCES

[14]   Kloe Kang, *Garden Eclipse: Ho'omaluhia*, 2001. 5 x 4 feet. Private collection.

[15]   Kloe Kang, *Bird of Paradise*, 2009. Charcoal and ink on paper. 25 x 36 inches. Private collection.

[16]   Adam LeBlanc, *Prevailing Winds*, 2019. Acrylic and mixed media panels. Eight panels, 16 x 20 inches each. Accompanied by eight poems by Joseph Stanton on placards. Collection of the artist.

[20]   Adam LeBlanc, *Nights on B Street*, 1993 and 2020. An installation consisting of seven mixed-media-diorama constructions, each 32 x 80 inches. The 2020 version is accompanied by eleven poems by Joseph Stanton on placards. Collection of the artist. Links to more information on the collaboration: <https://www.youtube.com/watch?v=cWwni__EwS8> <https://www.hawaii.edu/vice-versa/contents-summer-2021/stanton-leblanc/>

[28]   Chris Van Allsburg, *Just Desert*, illustration from his book *Mysteries of Harris Burdick* (Houghton Mifflin, 1984).

[29]   Sandy Bleiffer, *Paper Sculptures in Memory of What Happened in Hiroshima on 6 August 1945, 2006.*

[30]   Jackson Pollock, *Number 6*, 1949. Duco and aluminum paint on canvas. 44 × 54 inches. The Museum of Fine Arts, Houston, Texas.

[31]   Isamu Noguchi, *The Stone Within*, 1982. Basalt. The Isamu Noguchi Foundation and Garden Museum, Long Island City, New York.

[32]   Isamu Noguchi, *Brilliance*, 1982. Basalt. The Isamu Noguchi Foundation and Garden Museum, Long Island City, New York.

[34]   Isamu Noguchi, *Red*, 1965–66. Red Persian travertine. 64 x 23 x 22 inches. Honolulu Museum of Art, Honolulu, Hawai'i.

[35]   Francis Bacon, *Three Studies for a Self Portrait*, 1983. Oil on canvas. 14 x 12 inches. Honolulu Museum of Art, Honolulu, Hawai'i.

[36]   Edward Hopper, *Summertime*, 1943. Oil on canvas. 44 x 29 inches. Delaware Art Museum, Wilmington, Delaware.

[37]   George Ault depicted Russell's Corners—a site in Woodstock, New York—in a number of paintings he made toward the end of his life.

[38]   Winslow Homer, *The Sharpshooter on Picket Duty*, 1863. Oil on canvas. 12 x 16 inches. Portland Museum of Art, Portland, Maine.

[39]   Winslow Homer, *Home, Sweet Home*, 1863. Oil on canvas. 16 x 21 inches. National Gallery of Art, Washington, D.C.

[40]   Winslow Homer, *Croquet Scene*, 1866. Oil on canvas. 26 x 16 inches. Art Institute of Chicago, Chicago, Illinois.

[42]   Winslow Homer, *Artists Sketching in the White Mountains*, 1868. Oil on panel. 16 x 9 inches. Portland Museum of Art, Portland, Maine.

[43]   Winslow Homer, *The Bridle Path, White Mountains*, 1868. Oil on canvas. 38 x 24 inches. Clark Art Institute, Williamstown, Massachusetts.

[44]   Winslow Homer, *Summer Night*, 1890. Oil on canvas. 40 x 30 inches. Musée d'Orsay, Paris, France.

[45]   Winslow Homer, *Hurricane, Bahamas*, 1898. Watercolor and graphite on off-white wove paper. Metropolitan Museum of Art, New York City.

[46]   Thomas Cole, *Expulsion from the Garden of Eden*, 1828. Oil on canvas. 54 x 40 inches. Museum of Fine Arts, Boston, Massachusetts.

# ACKNOWLEDGMENTS

The author would like to thank the editors of the following publications in which these poems first appeared, often in different versions:

*ARTbeat*: "Sandy Bleiffer's Paper Sculptures in Memory of What Happened in Hiroshima on 6 August 1945"; ***The Asses of Parnassus***: "The Automatic Decay of André Breton's Corpse"; *Avocet*: "Driving Home Together on Valentine's Day"; ***Bamboo Ridge***: "Coffee Mānoa, Clouds Rising," "Finches at Dusk in the Treetops," "The Last Kaua'i 'O'o," "A Man Melted on Maunakea Street," "The Night of the 'A'o," "Philodoria," "Saffron Finches," "Saga Tree," "Sandalwood," and "Super Luminal Dithering"; ***Chaminade Literary Review***: "After Reading Kerouac" and "A Man Melted on Maunakea Street"; ***Cortland Review***: "For Sinatra in the Wee Small Hours"; ***Dreams and Nightmares***: "Moth Monologues"; ***Ekphrastic Review***: "Winslow Homer's *The Sharpshooter on Picket Duty*," "Winslow Homer's *Home Sweet Home*," "Winslow Homer's *Artists Sketching in the White Mountains*," "Winslow Homer's *Bridle Path, White Mountains*," and "Winslow Homer's *A Summer Night*"; ***Ekphrasis***: "Isamu Noguchi's *Brilliance*"; ***Hawai'i Pacific Review***: "Albatross," "Hala," "Kula Skylark," "Web of an Orb Weaver," and "White Ginger"; ***Journal of Wild Culture***: "Honeycreepers"; ***Kaimana***: "Kloe Kang's *Bird of Paradise*" and "Kloe Kang's *Garden Eclipse at Ho'omaluhia*"; ***Maine Review***: "Finches Roiling at Sunset" and "Frigate Bird"; ***Mississippi Review***: "Yorick Replies to Hamlet"; ***New Letters***: "Asbestos" and "Blue Marble Tree"; ***Pencil Marks***: "You're Right, We're Left, He's Gone"; ***Ricochet***: "The Koolau's After the Storm"; ***Third Wednesday***: "Ways of Disappearing"; ***Vice-Versa***: "Nights on B Street"; ***Walt's Corner***: "Isamu Noguchi's *Red*".

"After Reading Kerouac" also appeared in *For Jack: Poems for Jack Kerouac*, edited by George Wallace.

"Asbestos" and "Blue Marble Tree" also appeared in *Poetry Daily*, edited by Don Selby.

"For Frank Sinatra in the Wee Small Hours" also appeared in *Sinatra*, edited by Gilbert Gigliotti.

"Frigate Bird" also appeared in *Honolulu Weekly* and *Sunset Inn: Tales from the North Shore*.

"Sandy Bleiffer's Paper Sculptures in Memory of What Happened in Hiroshima on 6 August 1945" also appeared in Hiroshima/Nagasaki Memorial Project Catalog.

"Yorick Replies to Hamlet" also appeared in *Poets Speaking to Poets*, edited by Nicholas Fargnoli and Robert Hamblin.

"Honeycreepers" (a sequence of poems) was displayed as a set of broadsides at the Hoʻomaluhia Gallery.

"Adam LeBlanc's *Prevailing Winds*" (a sequence of poems) was displayed as a set of broadsides at Gallery ʻIolani in juxtaposition with LeBlanc's paintings.

"Adam LeBlanc's *Nights on B Street*" (a sequence of poems) was displayed as a set of broadsides at Gallery ʻIolani in juxtaposition with LeBlanc's installation.

# ABOUT THE AUTHOR

photo: Franklin Hayashida

Joseph Stanton's previous books of poems are *Moving Pictures, Things Seen, Imaginary Museum: Poems on Art, A Field Guide to the Wildlife of Suburban Oʻahu, Cardinal Points,* and *What the Kite Thinks: A Linked Poem* (co-authored with Makoto Ōoka, Wing Tek Lum, and Jean Toyama). His other books include *Looking for Edward Gorey, The Important Books: Children's Picture Books as Art and Literature,* and *Stan Musial: A Biography.* His poems have appeared in *Poetry, New Letters, Harvard Review, Antioch Review, New York Quarterly,* and many other magazines. As an art historian, Stanton has written about Winslow Homer, Edward Hopper, Edward Gorey, Maurice Sendak, and other American artists. He has collaborated with artists, musicians, and other writers and has received many awards for his work, including the Tony Quagliano International Poetry Award, the Cades Award for Literature, and the Ekphrasis Prize. Professor Emeritus of Art History and American Studies at the University of Hawaiʻi at Mānoa, he continues to teach in varied settings, most recently teaching the Starting with Art poetry workshop at Poets House in New York City and at the Honolulu Museum of Art.

# SHANTI ARTS

## NATURE · ART · SPIRIT

Please visit us online
to browse our entire book catalog,
including poetry collections and fiction,
books on travel, nature, healing, art,
photography, and more.

Also take a look at our highly regarded art
and literary journal, *Still Point Arts Quarterly*,
which may be downloaded for free.

www.shantiarts.com